THE

California
Cookbook

CALIFORNIA
Fresh

John P. Carroll

ILLUSTRATED BY
DARLENE CAMPBELL

Chronicle Books

First published in 1992 by
The Appletree Press Ltd,
7 James Street South, Belfast BT2 8DL.
Copyright © 1992 The Appletree Press, Ltd.
Illustrations © 1992 Darlene Campbell used
under Exclusive License to
The Appletree Press, Ltd.

First published in the United States in 1992 by
Chronicle Books, 275 Fifth Street,
San Francisco, CA 94103

ISBN 0-8118-0097-0

9 8 7 6 5 4 3 2 1

Introduction

California's style of cooking is steeped in history and imagination. To compile a list of 30 recipes from the state's impressive bounty was quite a task. I tried to tap not only the region's bounty, but its ethnic traditions, history, and modern innovations as well.

There is a marked difference between fancy California cuisine and the simple home cooking presented in this book. The recipes included here are for delicious food without frills. It's the kind of eating anyone can enjoy, due to modern transportation and an abundance of small farms yielding good produce. There really is no longer an "only in California" style of dining.

When it comes to freshness, Californians are certainly spoiled. The state produces half of the United States' supply of fruits, nuts, and vegetables on only three percent of the country's farmland. California is the sole domestic producer of almonds, artichokes, kiwifruit, figs, dates, olives, pistachios, pomegranates, prunes, and raisins, and leads the country in the growth of at least a dozen other crops.

The recipes in this collection best define California cooking because they are robust, inventive, and diverse, and are representative of a place where eating well is as common at a ball game as it is at home or in a restaurant.

A note on measures

Spoon measurements are level except where otherwise indicated. Seasonings can of course be adjusted according to taste. Recipes are for four, unless otherwise noted.

Apple Raisin Muffins

These moist muffins are substantial, and dense with apples, nuts, and raisins.

---

2 cups all-purpose flour
2 tsp baking powder
1 tsp cinnamon
$^1/_2$ tsp salt
$^1/_2$ cup sugar
2 eggs
1 cup milk
$^1/_3$ cup melted butter
1 $^1/_2$ cups chopped peeled apple
$^1/_2$ cup raisins
$^1/_2$ cup chopped walnuts
(makes 16)

Preheat the oven to 375°F and grease a muffin pan. Stir and toss together the flour, baking powder, cinnamon, and salt. In another bowl beat together the sugar, eggs, milk, melted butter, apple, raisins, and walnuts. Add the combined dry ingredients and beat just until the batter is blended. Spoon into the prepared muffin pan, filling each cup about two-thirds full. Bake for about 20 minutes, or until lightly browned and a toothpick inserted into the center of a muffin comes out clean. Let cool in the pans for a few minutes, then turn out onto racks. Serve warm.

Avocado, Mushroom and
Jack Cheese Omelet

Don't be afraid of omelet-making. The technique is quite simple and fast, and the cooking time only a minute or two. Have all the ingredients ready before you turn on the stove.

½ cup sliced mushrooms	3 eggs
2 tbsp butter	¼ cup diced avocado
salt	¼ cup finely grated
freshly ground black pepper	Monterey Jack cheese

(serves 1)

Cook the mushrooms in 1 tablespoon of the butter until tender. Season with salt and pepper; set aside.

Whisk the eggs briefly with ¼ teaspoon salt and a pinch of pepper. Set a nonstick skillet with a bottom diameter of about 8 inches over high heat and drop in the remaining tablespoon of butter, swirling the pan as the butter melts. In about 2 minutes, when the butter is very hot but has not browned, pour in the eggs. Let sit for about 10 seconds, then swirl the pan vigorously for about 10 seconds more. Stop, and with a spatula, lift some of the cooked egg at the edges, tilting the pan so the raw egg from the center flows underneath. When the eggs are nearly set but still creamy, scatter the cooked mushrooms, the avocado and cheese on one side. With a spatula, flip the other half over the filling. To serve, turn the pan upside down over a warm plate, letting the omelet fall bottom up.

Huevos Rancheros

"Rancher's eggs" come from early California Mexican land grants, which were called *rancheros*. There are many versions, though most are made with fresh *salsa* spooned over cooked eggs on flour tortillas, with a mild cheese sprinkled on top.

---

salsa *(see below)*
4 flour tortillas *(about 6 inches in diameter)*
8 poached eggs
2 cups grated Monterey Jack or Teleme cheese
fresh cilantro sprigs, or chopped parsley

Heat the *salsa* until barely warm. In an ungreased cast iron skillet or griddle (do *not* use a nonstick pan), heat the tortillas over high heat for several seconds on each side, until browned and blistered a little. Place a tortilla on each plate and spoon a couple tablespoons of salsa in the center. Top each with 2 eggs then spoon the remaining sauce over the tortillas and around the eggs. Sprinkle each with $1/2$ cup cheese. Place under a hot broiler for about 1 minute, until the cheese is melted. Garnish with cilantro sprigs or parsley and serve.

Salsa

More than an accompaniment to Mexican food and tortilla chips this excels with scrambled eggs, omelets, polenta, grilled chicken. It's a fresh-tasting, pleasantly sharp tomato sauce.

4 medium tomatoes	2 jalapeño peppers,
I red onion, finely chopped	seeded and minced
3 green onions, chopped	3 tbsp chopped cilantro
2 cloves garlic, minced	2 tbsp wine vinegar
	I tsp salt

(makes about 4 cups)

Chop the tomatoes coarsely and toss in a bowl with the red and green onions, garlic, jalapeños, cilantro, vinegar, and salt. Chill before serving.

Smoothy

A thick, cool, filling fruit and juice drink. You'll be surprised at how good it tastes first thing in the morning when you're in a hurry and want something substantial.

$^1/_2$ cup sliced strawberries	2 tbsp bran
3 ripe figs, 2 kiwifruit or an	I tbsp wheat germ, plain
additional $^1/_2$ cup strawberries	or toasted
$^1/_3$ cup orange juice	I – 2 tbsp honey
$^1/_3$ cup milk	2 ice cubes
2 tbsp nonfat dry milk	

(serves I)

Put all the ingredients in a blender and blend until smooth and frothy. Serve cold in a tall glass.

Guacamole

Good guacamole has small chunks of tomato and avocado and a rich, buttery flavor. Think of it as more than just a dip for tortilla chips, and spoon it on top of enchiladas, tacos, salads, and omelets.

---

3 large, ripe avocados
1 large tomato, peeled, seeded and chopped
1/4 cup (2 oz) canned diced mild green chillies
1 clove garlic, minced

3 tbsp fresh lime or lemon juice
2 tbsp chopped fresh cilantro
1 tsp salt
1/2 tsp freshly ground black pepper
tortilla chips

Peel and pit the avocados and mash them with a fork, but don't make the mixture too smooth. Stir in the tomato, chillies, garlic, lime or lemon juice, and cilantro. Season with salt and pepper. Place in a bowl and surround with tortilla chips.

Nachos

An informal dish of Mexican extraction. Though usually an appetizer, nachos are substantial enough to be a full meal. Serve them with beer or margaritas.

---

6 cups tortilla chips
2 cups warm refried beans
3 cups grated Monterey Jack cheese
1/2 cup chopped canned peeled green chillies

1/2 cup chopped green onion
sprigs of fresh cilantro, if desired
salsa, either homemade (see page 8) or bottled
sour cream, if you wish

Preheat the oven to 400°F. Spread the tortilla chips on a large pie pan or ovenproof platter. Spoon the beans over the chips but don't cover the chips completely. Toss the cheese, chillies, and onion together and scatter them over the beans. Bake for 5 – 10 minutes, until the cheese is melted and the dish is hot through. Garnish with cilantro and serve with salsa, and sour cream if you wish.

Lavosh

Lavosh, also known as Armenian cracker bread, is baked in thin, crisp plate-sized rounds. Serve it with soups and salads, or as an accompaniment to cheeses and dips. If your oven is small, bake the rounds in relays, like cookies.

1 package dry yeast,	*2 cups whole wheat flour*
about 2 1/2 tsp	*1 – 1 1/4 cups all-purpose flour*
1 1/2 cups warm water	*3 tbsp toasted sesame seeds*
2 tsp salt	

(makes 8)

Sprinkle the yeast over the water in a large bowl, stir, and let stand a few minutes. Add the salt and whole wheat flour and beat until blended. Add 1/2 cup of all-purpose flour, beating well, then add enough remaining flour to make a manageable dough. Knead on a lightly floured surface for about 10 minutes, adding a little more flour if necessary to keep it from being too sticky. Place in a greased bowl, cover and let rise about 1 hour, or until doubled in bulk. Punch down and let rise again until double. Divide into 8 equal pieces and roll each between your palms into a round ball. Cover and let rest for 20 minutes.

Preheat the oven to 450°F. On a floured surface roll each ball into an 8 − 9-inch circle. With the rolling pin, press a teaspoon of seeds into the surface of each. Place as many as will fit on a single layer on a large baking sheet and bake for 6 minutes. Turn the breads over and bake about 6 minutes more, until lightly browned. Cool on a rack before storing airtight.

Whole Grain Bread

This is a coarse-textured, nutritious, and satisfying loaf with an earthy taste.

---

2 cups warm water	3 tbsp vegetable oil
2 packages dry yeast	2 1/2 tsp salt
1/4 cup molasses	1/2 cup toasted wheat germ
1/4 cup brown sugar	1/2 cup toasted sunflower seeds
1/2 cup instant nonfat dry milk	4 − 5 cups whole wheat flour

(makes 2)

Stir the warm water and yeast together in a large bowl and let stand a few minutes. Stir in the molasses, brown sugar, dry milk, oil, and salt. Add the wheat germ, sunflower seeds and 2 cups of flour, and beat vigorously for 1 minute. Add enough of the remaining flour to make a manageable dough. Knead for 1 minute on a floured surface, then let rest for 10 minutes.

Resume kneading for about 10 minutes more, until smooth and elastic, adding enough additional flour to keep it from being too sticky. Place in a greased bowl, cover, and let rise until double.

Punch down and shape into two loaves. Place each in a greased 8 1/2 x 4 1/2 x 2 1/2-inch loaf pan. Cover loosely and let rise to the top of the pans. Bake in a preheated oven at 350°F for about 1 hour. Remove from the pans and cool on racks.

Wild Rice Salad

With increased California production, wild rice is affordable and more available than ever. It is best prepared simply, so don't overload this salad with too many ingredients.

4 cups cooked warm wild rice (1 cup raw rice)	1/2 cup chopped parsley
	1/2 cup chopped green onion
1/2 cup olive oil	2 tbsp chopped fresh mint
1/2 cup raisins	1 tomato, peeled, seeded and chopped
salt	
freshly ground black pepper	3 tbsp wine vinegar

(serves 6)

In a large bowl toss the rice with the olive oil and raisins. Season with 1 teaspoon salt and 1/2 teaspoon pepper and let cool to room temperature, tossing occasionally.

Add the parsley, green onion, mint, and tomato and toss to combine. Add the vinegar and toss. Taste, and add more salt, pepper, or vinegar if necessary. It should be flavorful but not overwhelmed with vinegar.

Cobb Salad

The best Cobb Salad is made with freshly prepared ingredients, carefully seasoned. This wonderful combination of flavors and textures was invented by Bob Cobb at Hollywood's Brown Derby Restaurant in 1936.

3/4 cup olive oil	2 cups finely diced cooked chicken breast
3 tbsp red wine vinegar	
salt	4 cups finely chopped iceberg lettuce
freshly ground black pepper	
2 hard-boiled eggs, peeled and chopped	2 cups chopped chicory or curly endive
2 tbsp chopped fresh parsley or chives	1 cup watercress sprigs
	1/2 cup crumbled blue cheese
2 large red, ripe tomatoes, peeled, seeded and diced	1 avocado, peeled and diced
	6 slices bacon, cooked crisp and crumbled

To make the dressing, combine the oil, vinegar, 1/2 teaspoon salt, and 1/4 teaspoon freshly ground pepper in a tightly capped jar and shake vigorously until blended; set aside.

In a small bowl toss the eggs with the parsley or chives, a sprinkling of salt and pepper and 2 tablespoons of dressing. In another bowl toss the tomatoes with 2 tablespoons of dressing and season with salt and pepper. In another bowl season the chicken with salt and pepper and toss with 2 tablespoons of dressing. In a large bowl toss together the lettuce, chicory, and watercress sprigs. Pour on the remaining dressing and toss to combine; season with salt and pepper to taste.

Spread the greens in a shallow mound on a large platter or salad bowl. Arrange the eggs, tomato, chicken, cheese, avocado, and bacon nicely on top. Take to the table and toss just before serving.

Chinese Chicken Salad

A chicken and noodle salad with Chinese overtones, this is very good and quick to make. It is an American invention, more for occidental palates than Asian.

---

1 1/2 tbsp soy sauce	1 large whole chicken breast, poached and cooled
2 tbsp peanut oil	
1 tbsp sesame oil	3 green onions, thinly sliced
1 tsp hot chilli oil	1 tbsp minced fresh ginger
1 1/2 tbsp rice wine vinegar	3 cups shredded iceberg lettuce
vegetable oil or peanut oil for frying	
	1/4 cup chopped toasted cashews
2 oz bean threads (available in Chinese markets)	sprigs of fresh cilantro

(serves 3 – 4)

To make the dressing, combine the soy sauce, oils, and vinegar in a tightly capped jar and shake vigorously; set aside for about 15 minutes.

In a wok or a large iron skillet heat 1/2 inch oil to 375°F. Add the bean threads a handful at a time — they will immediately puff and rise. Fry and toss gently for about 20 seconds, then drain on paper towels.

Remove the chicken from the bone and shred it. Toss with

the green onion, ginger, dressing, and one-third of the bean threads. Line a platter with the lettuce, sprinkle with the remaining bean threads, and spread the chicken mixture on top. Garnish with cashews and cilantro.

Spinach Salad with Goat Cheese

Salads combining hot and cold ingredients and a variety of textures are interesting to eat and usually easy to make. Wash and dry the spinach well, taking care not to bruise the leaves.

---

1 goat cheese log (about 5 oz)	$^1/_2$ tsp ground cumin
$^2/_3$ cup olive oil	salt
$^1/_3$ cup fine dry bread crumbs	freshly ground pepper
1 tbsp red wine vinegar	2 bunches fresh young spinach,
1 tsp Dijon-type mustard	washed, dried and stemmed

(serves 6)

Slice the goat cheese into six $^1/_2$-inch rounds. Pour 3 tablespoons of the olive oil in a small bowl. Dip each cheese round in the oil then roll in bread crumbs. Chill for 1 hour.

Preheat the oven to 375°F. In a small bowl whisk together the vinegar, mustard and cumin, then whisk in 4 tablespoons of the remaining oil. Season with salt and pepper.

Pour the last of the oil (about 3 tablespoons) in an 8-inch square baking pan. Set the prepared goat cheese in the dish and bake for about 8 minutes, until lightly browned.

Toss the spinach with the dressing and arrange on 6 salad plates. Place one cheese round in the center of each salad and serve immediately.

Gazpacho

A summer soup of Spanish influence, this is good for a barbecue or picnic, and is best made when tomatoes are red, ripe, and full of flavor.

---

1 1/2 lb tomatoes	3 tbsp olive oil
2 cloves garlic, minced	2 tbsp red wine vinegar
1 English cucumber, halved, seeded, and diced	1 1/2 cups, more or less, tomato juice
1 small red bell pepper, minced	salt
1 small red onion, minced	freshly ground black pepper
1 rib celery, minced	hot pepper sauce

(serves 6)

Peel the tomatoes and cut them in half horizontally. Working over a colander set in a bowl, scrape out most of the seeds and juices from the insides. Discard the seeds in the colander, but save the juice in the bowl. Chop the tomatoes finely and place them in the bowl with their juice. Add the garlic, cucumber, pepper, onion, and celery.

In another bowl whisk the oil and vinegar together then add 1 1/2 cups of tomato juice. Add to the vegetable mixture and stir to blend. If necessary, add more tomato juice to obtain a soupy consistency. Season with salt, pepper, and pepper sauce to taste, and chill thoroughly before serving.

Cold Avocado and Cucumber Soup

Bacon brings out the flavor of this fresh-flavored cold soup, which is good for a picnic or summer lunch.

---

2 tbsp olive oil
I onion, minced
2 cloves garlic, minced
3 medium avocados
2 cups, more or less, chicken stock
¹/₂ cup heavy cream
I English cucumber, peeled, seeded, and finely chopped
I tbsp lemon juice
salt
freshly ground black pepper
sour cream or plain yogurt
6 slices bacon, cooked crisp and crumbled
(makes 6 cups)

Heat the oil in a medium pan, add the onion and cook gently for 5 minutes. Add the garlic and cook I minute more; set aside.

Peel, pit and chop the avocados. Purée them in a food processor, then add 2 cups of stock and blend until smooth. Blend in the cream and the cooked onion mixture. Transfer to a bowl and stir in the cucumber and lemon juice. Season with salt and pepper. Chill thoroughly. If the soup seems too thick thin it with a little more stock. Top each bowl with a spoonful of sour cream or yogurt and sprinkle with bacon.

Shrimp-Stuffed Artichokes

An elegant dish — whole steamed artichokes with the thistle-like choke removed from the center and a delicate shrimp salad filling the hollow.

---

4 large artichokes, washed and trimmed
1 lb (about 2 cups) tiny cooked shrimp
2 tbsp chopped parsley
2 tbsp chopped fresh dill or tarragon
1 tbsp, or more, lemon juice
2 tbsp olive oil
1/2 cup mayonnaise
salt
freshly ground pepper

Wash and trim the artichokes. Steam them over boiling water in a covered kettle for 30 — 40 minutes, or until tender when pierced. Turn them bottoms up, place on paper towels, and chill thoroughly.

Carefully spread the center leaves of each artichoke open enough to expose the thistle-like choke. With a spoon, scoop and scrape the choke out, leaving the edible artichoke bottom intact. The artichoke should retain its shape, with a hole in the center for the filling.

Toss the shrimp with the parsley, dill or tarragon and 1 tablespoon lemon juice. Blend the oil and mayonnaise together, add to the shrimp mixture and toss to combine. Season with salt and pepper to taste and additional lemon juice if necessary. Fill the artichokes with the mixture and serve.

Chinese Almond Chicken

Quick to make and healthy, this stir-fry dish of chicken, crisply cooked vegetables, and toasted almonds is very good over rice.

I cup chicken stock
2 tbsp soy sauce
I tbsp cornstarch
2 tbsp vegetable oil or peanut oil
4 celery stalks, thinly sliced diagonally
2 skinless, boneless chicken breast halves, cut in thin strips
I cup thinly sliced mushrooms
I cup bean sprouts
4 green onions, thinly sliced
$^1/_2$ cup chopped, toasted almonds
salt
freshly ground pepper

Stir the stock, soy sauce, and cornstarch together until blended; set aside. In a large, heavy skillet, or in a wok, heat the oil over high heat until it is smoking hot. Do not leave the pan unattended. Add the celery and cook briskly, stirring and tossing constantly, for about 2 minutes.

Add the chicken and mushrooms and continue cooking over high heat, tossing and stirring constantly, for 2 – 3 minutes more, until the chicken is cooked through.

Stir up the stock mixture and add it to the chicken along with the bean sprouts, green onion, and almonds and cook about I minute more, until thickened. Season with salt and pepper. Serve over rice.

Shrimp and Sun-dried Tomato Pizza

California is the birthplace of many innovative pizzas — the perfect food for casual dining. The topping suggestions here are guidelines, so feel free to experiment with what you've got on hand, including other cheeses, herbs, and vegetables.

Dough	Topping
1 package dry yeast	¹/₂ lb mushrooms, thinly sliced
1¹/₃ cups warm water	3 tbsp olive oil
4 cups, more or less,	2 cups tomato sauce
all-purpose flour	²/₃ cup oil-pack sun-dried
¹/₃ cup cornmeal	tomatoes, chopped
2 teaspoons salt	1 lb Teleme cheese, thinly sliced
¹/₄ cup olive oil	2 tbsp chopped fresh tarragon
	1 lb (2 cups) small
	cooked shrimp
	2 tbsp chopped parsley

(makes 2 12–14 inch pizzas)

To make the dough, sprinkle the yeast over the warm water in a large bowl and let stand a few minutes. Add 3 cups of flour, the cornmeal, salt and oil, and beat until smooth. Add about ¹/₂ cup more flour, to make a manageable dough. Knead on a floured surface for 10 minutes, sprinkling on additional flour as necessary to keep it from being too sticky. Place in a greased bowl, cover, and let rise until double. Punch the dough down and divide in half; let rest for about 10 minutes. Preheat the oven to 450°F. Patiently pat, roll, and stretch each piece of dough into a circle 12 — 14 inches across. Place each on a greased cookie sheet or pizza pan. Fold the outside edge in slightly to make a small rim. Prick the surface several times with a fork.

Toss the mushrooms with the oil and set aside. Spread 1 cup of tomato sauce on each round of dough, then dot each with 1/3 cup sun-dried tomatoes. Divide the mushrooms evenly over the pizzas, then the cheese. Bake 15 minutes, either on the lowest shelf of an electric oven or on the floor of a gas oven. Remove from the oven and rapidly sprinkle each pizza with the tarragon and shrimp. Bake 5 – 10 minutes more, until golden and bubbly. Sprinkle with the parsley, cut in wedges and serve.

Marinated Dungeness Crab

Though messy to eat, tossing cooking Pacific Dungeness crab meat in olive oil and lemon juice brings out its flavor, making it even sweeter. Serve with mayonnaise, lemon wedges, and plenty of paper napkins. You will also save time if you buy the crabs cooked, and have the fish market — which should cook them freshly and keep them on ice — clean and crack them.

1/2 cup olive oil	1/2 tsp salt
2 tbsp lemon juice	1/4 tsp freshly ground pepper
2 tbsp chopped fresh tarragon or parsley	2 large crabs, cooked, cleaned and well cracked

In a large bowl whisk together until completely blended the olive oil, lemon juice, tarragon or parsley, salt and pepper. Be sure the crab claws are well cracked so the marinade will penetrate the shells, and cut each body half into 2 pieces.

Toss the crabs with the marinade and refrigerate one hour before serving, tossing 2 or 3 times more.

Polenta with Teleme Cheese and Sausages

Creamy polenta, of northern Italian origins, is no more than fancy cornmeal mush, and just as easy to cook as hot cereal. It makes a satisfying dinner, goes beautifully with all kinds of additions and variations, and takes only minutes to make.

---

3 cups water
salt
$^3/_4$ cup cornmeal or polenta (coarse-ground cornmeal)
4 tbsp butter
$^1/_2$ cup, or more, cream or milk
$^1/_2$ lb cooked link sausage or Italian sausage
$1^1/_2$ cups (8 oz) diced Teleme cheese
freshly ground black pepper

Bring the water and 1 teaspoon salt to a boil in a large, heavy saucepan, preferably nonstick. Slowly pour in the cornmeal, whisking constantly, then cook and stir over low heat for about 5 minutes, until thickened. Continue cooking over lowest heat for about 10 minutes more, stirring frequently, until quite thick. Stir in the butter and $^1/_2$ cup cream or milk.

While the polenta cooks, cut the sausages crosswise into $^1/_4$-inch pieces. Heat the oil in a skillet and cook the pieces for about 5 minutes, tossing frequently, until lightly browned. Drain on paper towels, then stir into the polenta along with the cheese. Season with salt and pepper to taste. The mixture should be creamy; if necessary stir in a little more milk or cream.

Grilled Snapper with Cilantro Butter

Flavored butters, which keep well in the freezer, add savor to simple grilled foods. Don't worry if you can't get snapper, because almost any firm-textured fish takes well to this treatment.

Cilantro butter
$1/2$ cup butter, at room temperature
2 tbsp finely chopped fresh cilantro
I tsp finely grated lemon peel
I tbsp lemon juice
salt
freshly ground pepper
Fish
4 (about 8 oz each) snapper filets, about I inch thick
salt
freshly ground pepper
3 tbsp vegetable oil

To make the cilantro butter, in a small bowl beat the butter until smooth. Beat in the cilantro, lemon peel, and juice, then season with salt and pepper to taste. Mound on waxed paper and shape the mixture into a 4-inch log. Wrap well and chill until firm. To serve, cut into 8 half-inch slices.

Prepare a barbecue fire and position a grilling rack 4 – 6 inches from the heat. Sprinkle the fish lightly with salt and pepper and rub with oil. Grill for 8 – l0 minutes, turning once, or until the fish is cooked through. Transfer to warm plates and place a slice or two of cilantro butter on each serving.

Grilled Tuna

Tuna is a firm fish, rich tasting and ideal for grilling — and it isn't overwhelmed by this assertive marinade with Asian overtones.

---

¹/₄ cup soy sauce
2 tbsp rice vinegar or wine vinegar
2 tbsp shoah sing wine or dry sherry
I tbsp sesame oil
I tbsp freshly grated ginger root
I clove garlic, minced
4 (6 — 8 oz each) tuna or albacore steaks, about I inch thick
2 tbsp vegetable oil
lemon wedges

Whisk together the soy sauce, vinegar, wine, sesame oil, ginger root, and garlic. Arrange the fish in a single layer in a large, shallow glass or enamel baking dish and pour in the soy marinade. Refrigerate 2 — 3 hours, turning the fish once or twice.

Prepare a barbecue fire and place the grilling rack 4 — 6 inches from heat. Remove the fish from the marinade and pat it dry; reserve the marinade. Rub the fish with oil. Grill for 8 — 10 minutes, until cooked through, turning once and brushing 2 or 3 times with the reserved marinade. Transfer to warm plates and garnish with lemon wedges.

Strawberry Tart

Cooking some of the berries for the foundation of the tart and topping it with the remaining whole berries is a dandy way to preserve the essence and fresh taste of the fruit.

Tart dough	Filling
I cup all-purpose flour	6 cups strawberries, cleaned
I tbsp sugar	and hulled
1/4 tsp salt	1/2 tbsp cornstarch
1/2 cup (I stick) chilled butter,	1/3 cup sugar
cut in bits	I tbsp lemon juice
I tsp water	1/4 cup currant jelly
	I cup heavy cream

(makes I 9-inch tart)

To make the tart shell, combine the flour, sugar, salt, and butter in a food processor. Process several seconds, until the mixture looks like fine, dry crumbs. Add the water and process a few seconds longer, until it forms a cohesive ball. Pat into a small cake, wrap tightly and chill about 30 minutes.

Preheat the oven to 425°F. Roll out the dough on a floured surface and fit it into a 9-inch tart pan. Prick all over with a fork then press a piece of heavy-duty foil snugly into the shell. Bake for 8 minutes, then remove the foil and bake about 8 minutes longer, until lightly browned. Cool completely before filling.

To make the filling, remove I cup of the berries, taking the small or imperfect ones, and crush them. Combine the cornstarch and 1/4 cup of the sugar in a saucepan. Add the crushed berries and lemon juice and cook over medium heat,

stirring constantly, until it thickens. Cool to room temperature.

Spread the berry mixture in the tart shell. Arrange the whole berries on top. Bring the currant jelly to a boil and brush a thin coating over the berries and the rim of the crust. Whip the cream with the remaining sugar (about 2 tablespoons). Spoon some around the edge of the tart and pass the remainder at the table.

Peach Shortcake

Don't get in a strawberry rut with summery shortcake. Sweetened peaches, macerated in a little rum and flecked with kiwifruit, dress up this plain dessert and give it a decidedly adult flavor.

6 – 8 large ripe peaches	**Shortcake**
1/3 cup rum or brandy	2 cups all-purpose flour
1/4 cup sugar	1/4 cup sugar
2 kiwifruit, peeled and thinly	1 tbsp baking powder
sliced, if desired	1/2 tsp salt
	1 1/4 cups, or more, heavy cream
	sweetened whipped cream

(serves 6)

Peel, pit and thinly slice the peaches. Toss them in a bowl with the rum and sugar and let stand 30 minutes, tossing occasionally. Add the kiwifruit, if you wish, and toss to combine; set aside.

Preheat the oven to 425°F. For the shortcake, in a bowl stir and toss together the flour, sugar, baking powder, and salt. Add 1 1/4 cups of cream and stir vigorously with a fork. The dough should be cohesive; if it is too dry, add a little more cream to make it hold together. On a lightly floured surface knead gently about 10 times, then pat into a circle about 6 inches across and ½-inch thick; place on a baking sheet. Bake for 25 – 30 minutes, until lightly browned and puffy. While still warm, split the cake horizontally. Place the bottom on a large platter. Spoon the fruit and its liquid on top and spread with a large blob of sweetened whipped cream. Set the top layer in place. Pass additional whipped cream at the table.

Citrus Compôte

A colorful, bittersweet compôte of orange, lemon, lime, and grapefruit. It is good warm or cold, either by itself or with crisp cookies and vanilla ice cream.

---

1 orange	2 cups sugar
1 grapefruit	2 cups water
1 lemon	1 cinnamon stick
1 lime	
(serves 6)	

Halve each of the citrus fruits lengthwise (through the stem), then cut crosswise into thin slices – about ⅛-inch – so they are half-moon shaped. Pick out any seeds. Drop all the fruit into a large pot of rapidly boiling water, return to a boil and boil for 3 minutes. Drain well, rinse with cold water and drain again; set aside.

Combine the sugar, water and cinnamon stick in a large saucepan and bring to a boil. Add the prepared fruit. Return to a boil, then reduce the heat and simmer gently for about 1½ hours, until the fruit is tender and the liquid has reduced

to a rather thick syrup. Serve warm or chilled. This keeps well in the refrigerator.

Churros

These long ropes of fried cream puff dough rolled in cinnamon sugar are a staple in Mexican bakeries. They are perfect for Sunday breakfast, and so satisfying you can't get enough of them.

½ cup water	4 eggs
½ cup milk	2 tsp vanilla
½ tsp salt	oil for frying
½ cup (4 oz) butter	¾ cup sugar
1 cup all-purpose flour	1 tbsp cinnamon

(makes 24)

Combine the water, milk, salt, and butter in a heavy saucepan. Heat slowly until the butter melts, then bring to a boil. Add the flour then cook over medium heat for about 3 minutes, beating constantly. Remove from heat and add the eggs one at a time, beating furiously after each until the mixture is smooth. Beat in the vanilla.

Heat about 2 inches of oil in a skillet to 390°F. Combine the sugar and cinnamon on a plate and set aside. Scoop the egg mixture into a pastry bag fitted with a ½-inch round or star tip. Squeeze the bag over the hot oil, pushing out a rope of paste about 4 inches long, then cut it off with a knife, letting it drop gently into the oil. Rapidly form 4 more churros the same way. Turn them frequently until golden, about 2 minutes. Remove with a slotted spoon and drain on paper towels.

While still warm, roll in cinnamon sugar. Fry and finish the remaining paste the same way.

Coffee Toffee Pie

A chocolate and coffee-flavored candy-like pie from Blum's, a long-gone haven for sweet lovers in San Francisco.

Crust
1 cup all-purpose flour
1/2 cup butter, softened
1/4 cup brown sugar
1 square (1 oz) unsweetened chocolate, grated
2 tbsp, or more, milk
3/4 cup finely chopped walnuts
Filling
1/2 cup butter, softened
3/4 cup sugar
2 tsp powdered instant coffee
1 square (1 oz) unsweetened chocolate, melted
2 eggs
Topping
1 1/2 cups chilled heavy cream
6 tbsp confectioners' sugar
1 1/2 tbsp nonfat dry milk
1 1/2 tbsp powdered instant coffee
1 tbsp grated unsweetened chocolate

(makes 1 9-inch pie)

Preheat the oven to 375°F. To make the crust, combine the flour, butter, brown sugar, and chocolate in a food processor and blend until crumbly. Add 2 tablespoons of milk and the walnuts and process until the dough forms a cohesive mass. If necessary, add a few drops more milk. Take walnut-sized pieces of the dough and press them into a 9-inch pie pan, preferably glass, covering the bottom and sides completely and evenly. Crimp the edges and prick the dough all over with

a fork. Press a piece of heavy-duty foil snugly into the pie shell and bake for 8 minutes. Remove the foil and bake about 10 minutes longer, or until dry and crisp. Cool completely.

To make the filling, beat the butter in the large bowl of an electric mixer until fluffy. Beating on high speed, gradually add the sugar, then the instant coffee and melted chocolate. Add 1 egg and beat on highest speed for 5 minutes. Add the second egg and beat 5 minutes more. Spread evenly in the pie shell then cover and refrigerate for several hours.

For the topping, combine the cream, confectioners' sugar, dry milk and instant coffee and beat until stiff. Spread over the pie and sprinkle with the grated chocolate. Refrigerate again for at least an hour before serving.

Jalapeño Jelly

This is a moderately hot jelly, and in California cocktail tradition is good served with softened cream cheese as a spread for crackers. It also goes well with smoked fish and poultry.

---

1 green bell pepper	1 cup cider vinegar
(about 1/2 lb)	1 tsp salt
1/2 lb jalapeño peppers	1 2-oz box powdered pectin
2 cups water	4 cups sugar

(makes 2 pints)

Remove the stems from all the peppers. Grind the peppers coarsely or chop them in a food processor.

Combine the chopped peppers with the water, vinegar, and salt in a saucepan, bring to a boil, then reduce the heat and simmer for 15 minutes. Pour into a colander lined with several thicknesses of cheesecloth and let drain into a bowl, pressing gently to extract the juice.

Discard the pulp and measure 3 cups of the extracted pepper juice. If you are short, add a little water. Pour into a saucepan of at least 6-quart capacity. Add the pectin and stir a few minutes to dissolve. Place over high heat and bring to a boil, stirring constantly. Stir in the sugar, then bring back to a full rolling boil and boil exactly 2 minutes more, stirring constantly. Remove from the heat and rapidly skim off any foam. Pour into hot, sterilized jars and seal.

Red Wine Barbecue Sauce

A light, moderately spicy barbecue sauce, good brushed on chicken, veal, or beef every 20 minutes while cooking.

1/4 cup vegetable oil	2 tbsp sugar
I onion, finely chopped	1/2 tsp red pepper flakes
I cup dry red wine	grated zest of I lime or lemon
1/2 cup red wine vinegar	1/2 tsp salt
2 tbsp white wine Worcestershire sauce, or plain Worcestershire sauce	

(makes about 2 cups)

Heat the oil in a saucepan, add the onion and cook gently about 5 minutes. Add the wine, vinegar, Worcestershire sauce, sugar, red pepper flakes, lime or lemon zest, and salt. Bring to a boil, reduce the heat and simmer, partially covered, for 15 minutes. Cool and refrigerate, tightly covered.

Drinks

Shakes You'd be apt to find one of these creamy, sweet, fruity milkshakes roadside diners. In the Southern California desert, which produces the entire United States' supply of dates, you'll find them made from dates.

---

the flesh from any desired fruit or 10 large pitted dates
³/₄ cup milk
1 tsp vanilla extract
2 scoops vanilla ice cream
(serves 1)

Chop the fruit finely by hand and place in a blender. Add 2 – 3 tablespoons of milk and blend until smooth. Add the remaining milk, the vanilla and the ice cream and whirl briefly just until blended. Serve immediately in a tall glass.

White Wine Spritzer: Plain spritzers aren't very interesting. This version is a little fancier, and tastes much better, I think.

1½ tsp sugar	½ cup sparkling water or
1½ tbsp orange juice	club soda, more or less
½ cup dry white wine	1 thin orange slice
ice cubes	
(serves 1)	

Combine the sugar, orange juice, and wine and stir until the sugar is dissolved. Pour over ice cubes in a tall glass, then fill the glass with sparkling water. Garnish with the orange slice.

Index

Apple Raisin Muffins 4
Avocado, Mushroom and
  Jack Cheese Omelet 7

Chinese Almond
  Chicken 32
Chinese Chicken Salad 23
Churros 51
Citrus Compôte 48
Cobb Salad 20
Coffee Toffee Pie 52
Cold Avocado and
  Cucumber Soup 28

Gazpacho 27
Grilled Snapper with
  Cilantro Butter 40
Grilled Tuna 43
Guacamole 12

Huevos Rancheros 8

Jalapeño Jelly 55

Lavosh 15

Marinated Dungeness
  Crab 36

Nachos 12

Peach Shortcake 47
Polenta with Teleme
  Cheese and Sausages 39

Red Wine Barbecue
  Sauce 56

Salsa 8
Shakes 59
Shrimp and Sun-dried
  Tomato Pizza 35
Shrimp-Stuffed
  Artichokes 31
Smoothy 11
Spinach Salad with Goat
  Cheese 24
Strawberry Tart 44

White Wine Spritzer 59
Whole Grain Bread 16
Wild Rice Salad 19